Complete Guide to Platy Fish

*Comprehensive Guide on Platy Fish Pet
Health care, Aquarium set up, Breeding,
Tank mates, Feeding and lots more*

Wales Kevin

book provided, but they are unable to guarantee its accuracy to doctors advice, completeness, or timeliness. This guide's contents might change at any time and without prior warning.

For individualized advice and direction tailored to your unique situation, please speak with a licensed veterinarian or knowledgeable fish keeper. Any loss or damage sustained as a direct or indirect consequence of the use, use, or interpretation of the information provided in this handbook is not the responsibility of the author or publisher.

TABLE OF CONTENTS

CHAPTER 1

INTRODUCTION

1.1 The History and Origins of Platy Fish

The ancient freshwater environments of Central America are where platy fish first appeared and where their history may/can be found. According to fossil evidence seen, platy fish have undergone several evolutionary changes over millions of years. The Poeciliidae family, which also contains well-known aquarium fish like guppies and swordtails, includes these tiny, vibrant known fish.

Early explorers and naturalists who traveled to Mexico, Guatemala, and Honduras in the 19th [nineteenth] century are credited with discovering and documenting the first platy fish ever. Aquarists and scientists alike were instantly drawn in by their distinctive look and brilliant colors they give off.

The phrase "Platy fish" comes from the Greek words "xiphos" which means "swords" and "phoros" which means "bearers," alluding to the male's extended anal fin. Its scientific name, Xiphophorus maculatus, which is derived/gotten from these concepts. However, diverse color variants and patterns of this fish have developed throughout time via selective breeding and hybridization, giving rise to several Platy fish strains and kinds out there.

Native to Central America Region, platy fish are most common in the warm, still waters of Mexico's rivers, streams, and marshes. The Yucatan Peninsula, the Gulf of Mexico's coastal regions, as well as portions of Guatemala and Honduras, are all included location in their large distribution zone. Platy fish may/can be seen swimming amid water plants in their native environments (wild), where they eat tiny invertebrates, algae, and plant detritus as feed.

Early in the 20th [twentieth] century, platy fish became more and more popular as aquarium pets. Their vivid colors, calm personalities, and generally simple maintenance needs enthralled aquarists and people. Due to the breeding and propagation of platy fish in captivity [owned as pet], the aquarium trade now has access to a wide range of color variants and patterns of them.

Different Platy fish strains were created mostly as a result of selective type breeding. Breeders concentrated more on improving desirable characteristics such pattern variety, fin form, and color intensity of them. A variety of Platy fish types, such as the Red Wagtail, Mickey Mouse, Tuxedo, and the well-known Wagtail and Pineapple kinds, have arisen through years of meticulous breeding process.

Researchers and scientists have also researched platy fish in great seen detail. For the study of behavior, reproductive biology, and genetics, they have been used as a model organism as they provide excellent study subjects/form for studying fish reproduction and genetic inheritance because to their ease of reproduction and live-bearing fry traits.

Concern for the preservation of natural Platy fish populations has grown in recent years. Threats to their natural environments include habitat degradation, pollutions, and the introduction of non-native species to them. Along with educational initiatives to increase awareness of the significance of Platy fish to the ecology part, conservation measures have been launched to conserve and maintain their natural habitats until date.

Future prospects show that platy fish will remain a popular species in the aquarium industry. Both novice, beginners and expert aquarists like them because to their beauty, versatility, and simplicity of maintenance. New and intriguing Platy fish variations are anticipated to emerge as a result of ongoing breeding operations and genetic developments, greatly enhancing the fish species' variety

1.2 Anatomy and Physical Characteristics

The Poeciliidae fish family includes tiny freshwater fish like the platy fish

(Xiphophorus maculatus). The platy fish has the following important anatomical details and physical characteristics (appearance):

1. Size: Although certain species may grow significantly bigger than the other, platy fish normally reach a length of 2.5-3 inches (6-7.5 cm).

2. Platy fish have an elongated, laterally compressed body that is flattened from side to side like that of a discus. They have a triangular-shaped head and an abdomen that is relatively rounded.

3. Color: Platy fish come in a variety of colors and hues, including solid firm colors, metallic tones, and other different patterns. Red, orange, yellow, blue, black, and white are common hues of platy. On their body, they might have spots or patches shown.

4. Fins: On the top of their bodies, platy fish have a single type dorsal fin. Males often have a bigger and longer dorsal fin than females do have. Additionally, they have pectoral fins, pelvic fins, and an anal fin for their swimming and navigating.

5. Livebearers: Platy fish give birth to live fry (new born) rather than eggs

like other fishes because they are livebearers. The fertilized eggs are carried within the female platy, who afterwards gives birth to fully developed fry platy. They are renowned for having a high rate of reproduction success.

6. Mouth and Teeth: The platy fish's tiny mouth is situated straight on the bottom of its head. They have tiny, sharp teeth's for scraping up algae and other microscopic creatures off surfaces of the water.

7. Eyes: The sides of the heads of platy fish are home to their big, white, spherical eyes. They can see well and

in many different directions from a spot, which aids in their ability to see predators and locate food faster.

8. Lateral Line: Platy fish, like the majority of fish out there, have a sensory system known as the lateral line which they can use to traverse their surroundings and find prey with the aid of this organ, which spans the length of their bodies and aids them in detecting slight vibrations and changes in water pressure.

9. Scales: To defend itself, a platy fish's body is coated with tiny, overlapping scales. The fish's overall appearance is influenced by the scales,

which can reflect light and are often iridescent adding to their appearance.

10. Active swimmers: Platy fish like to live in the middle and upper levels of the aquarium/tank. Compared to several other fish species, they are not so powerful swimmers.

These are a few of the general characteristics of platy fish , remember that there are several strains and color variants within the platy fish pet species, giving rise to a diverse range of looks.

1.3 Varieties of Platy Fish

1. Red Wagtail Platy: This variation has a black *"wagtail"* pattern on the tail fin and a red or orange like body.

2. Mickey Mouse Platy: Identified by its black body, which contrasts with a black like mark on the caudal peduncle and a black spot on the dorsal fin.

3. Tuxedo Platy: This species is named for its black body and fins, which resemble a tuxedo cloth. The body color may vary and might include reddish, orangey, yellowish, or blue type hues.

4. Sunset Platy: Exhibits vivid hues, such as hues of orange, red, and yellow

colors, sometimes with a metallic or iridescent shine on them.

5. Marigold platy: Mostly yellow with orange undertones, giving with uniform or patterned coloring.

6. Variatus Platy: These fish, which are related closely to common platies, exhibit a broader variety of hues and patterns, including blends of red color, orange, yellow, blue, and black.

7. Pineapple Platy: A distinctive pattern with a light yellow or beige body type hue and sporadic black spots or blotches that resembles the skin of a pineapple fruit.

8. Blue platy: This species has a blue body hue that ranges from a light sky blue color to a deep cobalt blue.

9. Wagtail Blue Platy: This species resembles the Red Wagtail Platy but has a different blue body instead of a red or orange one.

10. Coral platy: This colorful fish has a body that ranges in hue from pale pink to dark reddish pink color.

11. Gold Twinbar Platy: Has an eye-crossing black bar across their body

and a black bar close to the caudal peduncle.

12. Panda Platy: Displays a black body with white or light-colored spots on their body that resemble the coloring of a panda.

13. Redtail Platy: This variation of platy has a body that is mostly silver and a tail that is either bright red or orange in color.

14. Salt and Pepper Platy: Usually black or dark gray color on a lighter background hue, with a speckled or peppered pattern across their body.

15. Moon Platy: This platy has a shiny silver or gold like body with a circular or crescent-shaped pattern on the caudal peduncle, giving it its name for the moon-like pattern.

16. Neon Platy: This species is distinguished by its vivid neon coloring, which is often a mix of fluorescent blue, green, orange, or yellow.

17. Calico platy: This species is distinguished by areas of orange, red, black, and white coloration.

18. Panda Mickey Mouse Platy: This toy has the classic black and white

panda design together with the colour of a Mickey Mouse Platy.

19. High-Fin Platy: Resembling typical platies in appearance, but with longer, more pronounced fins, especially the dorsal fin.

20. Metallic platy: Displays a bright, metallic sheen on the body, often in shades of bronze, silvers, or gold.

1.4 Why Choose Platy Fish as Pets?

People chose platy fish as pets for a variety of reasons, including:

- Brilliant Colors: Platy fish are an eye-catching addition to any aquarium put in because to their broad variety of brilliant colors and patterns.

- Placid Nature: Platy fish are perfect for community tanks with other fishes because of their typically placid nature and ability to cohabit with a range of other peaceful community fishes.

- Simple Maintenance: Platy fish are good for beginning fish keepers since they are regarded as resilient and quite adaptable. They can handle a variety of water conditions and are quite simple to care for as pets.

- Active Swimmers: Platies are brisk, spirited swimmers that provide motion and life to the aquarium put in. They are entertaining to see and provide for an interesting experience in your home.

- Live bearing Reproduction: Platy fish give birth to live fry (newborn) rather than eggs since they are livebearers. The development of a new generation of fish in the aquarium may result from this reproductive activity, which is very interesting to see.

Platies are an excellent option for fish keepers with limited room or those just starting out since they can flourish in tiny tanks sizes.

- Educational Value: Keeping platy fish as pets, particularly for young children, may/can be educational. They may see the birth and development of the fry slowly and get knowledge about the livebearer life cycle.

- Algae limit: Platies eat algae as part of their diet/meal, which may help limit algae development in the aquarium and promote a healthy ecology in the tank space.

CHAPTER 2: SETTING UP THE PERFECT PLATY FISH TANK

2.1 Selecting an Aquarium

There are a few crucial elements to take into proper account while choosing an aquarium for platy fish:

1. The size of the aquarium:

Platies are little fish, but they still require quite a room to move about in. A common rule of thumb is to give each platy fish with at least 10(ten) liters of water. The greater the room you can provide for them, however, the better the swimming area and water quality will be for them.

Platies are aggressive swimmers, thus a rectangular or square-shaped tank is advised for them over a tall or spherical one. The length of the tank is very crucial since it provides the fish with enough of swimming room.

2. Filtration:

For platy fish to remain healthy and the water, quality in their tanks to be maintained, good filtration is very essential. Select a filter that offers mechanical and biological type filtration and is suitable for the tank's size you use. As platies like a modest water movement, a filter with adjustable flow rate is quite appropriate for this job.

3. Heating and Temperature:

Platies are tropical fish that need a constant temperature between 71 and 81 degrees Fahrenheit (about 22 and 28 degrees Celsius). Maintaining the proper temperature in the tank requires a dependable aquarium heater and thermometer.

4. Substrate and Decorations:

Because platies are not very sensitive to the kind of substrate you put, you have a variety of possibilities to choose. The best substrates to use are gravel or sand. To establish a natural atmosphere and offer the fish a feeling of security, provide some hiding spots for them, such as caves, plants, and driftwood.

5. **illumination**:

For platy fish, a modest amount of illumination is quite adequate. To improve the aesthetics and offer more hiding places, live plants may/can be placed to the fish tank. To avoid excessive algae development in the tank, take into account employing low to moderate intensity illuminations.

Platies can survive in a variety of water conditions, but it is crucial to keep the parameters all steady. Aim for a hardness (GH) of 8~12 dGH and a pH range of 7.0~8.2.

8. Tank Companions (tank mate):

Platies get along well with other calm communal fish. Avoid species that are aggressive or have fin nipping behaviors. Other calm livebearers, tetras, calm barbs, and tiny bottom-dwelling fish like corydoras catfish make good platy fish tank mates.

Before adding platy fish, remember to cycle the aquarium correctly to provide a stable and healthy habitat for your pet fish. A well balanced diet, periodic water testing, and partial regular water changes will all contribute to the platy fish's continued health in the tank.

2.2 Water Parameters and Filtration

Water Parameters for Platy Fish:

1. Temperature:

Platies like temperatures between 72°F and 82°F (22°C and 28°C). Their health and activity levels are all properly maintained when the water is kept in this range.

2. pH Level:

Platies may live in a broad variety of water pH values, although they prefer slightly alkaline environments to strive in. Try to maintain a pH between 7.0 and 8.2 in their tank.

3. Hardness:

Platies can adapt to a range of water hardness conditions. For their wellbeing, a general hardness (GH) of 8~12 dGH is ideal.

4. Nitrite and Ammonia:

In the aquarium, nitrite and ammonia should both be maintained/kept at undetectable levels. These substances are unhealthy for fish and may cause stress and illness to them. Low ammonia and nitrite levels need regular water testing and effective filtration to be kept.

5. Nitrate:

A byproduct of the nitrogen cycle in aquariums, nitrate may build up in the tank over time. To save the platies from any stress and possible health problems, keep the nitrate levels below 40 ppm by doing frequent partial water changes [about 25-30%].

Platy fish filtration:

1. Mechanical Filtration: To eliminate trash, uneaten food, and debris from the tank water, an effective filtration

system must use mechanical filtration. Filter floss, sponges, or filter pads are often used to do this filtration method.

2. Biological Filtration: Platies create ammonia as waste product, much as other fish do. The nitrogen cycle requires biological filtration to transform any ammonia into less dangerous compounds. To carry out this process, beneficial bacteria invade the substrate and filter medium. Make sure there is enough surface area in the filtering system used for the development of healthy bacteria.

3. Flow Rate: Platies love water with moderate movement, so choose a slow

filter with a variable flow rate or think about including a flow control mechanism to modify the flow as necessary. The fish may be stressed or have trouble swimming if the water flow is too fast or intense.

4. Consistent Maintenance: Consistent maintenance is necessary for proper filtration. To avoid clogging and guarantee peak performance, clean or replace filter media as necessary. To preserve water quality and get rid of accumulated garbage, regular water changes are also essential.

Your platy fish should live in a flourishing habitat if you maintain proper water parameters and ensure effective filtration is done. Their health depends on regular water quality monitoring and preventative maintenance.

2.3 Choosing Substrate and Decorations

The following elements should be taken into account while choosing a substrate and accessories for a platy fish aquarium:

1. Substrate: Gravel is a popular option for platy fish aquariums as a substrate. Because tiny particles might trap the debris, use a size that is not too small. Avoid pebbles with jagged edges since they could hurt the fish and select hues that enhance the tank's overall look.

- Sand is an additional choice for substrate used in fish tanks. Sand might be more straightforward to maintain and offers a natural look in the tank. To avoid creating anaerobic pockets in the substrate, use a fine-grained sand that won't compress too tightly.

- Plant Substrate: If you want to keep live plants in your platy fish tank, you may want to use a substrate made just for plants. These substrates often provide vital nutrients that will help support the development of plants.

2. Accents: - Plants Live or fake plants have several advantages for your platy fish aquariums. Live plants give fish hiding places, oxygen flow, and assistance in maintaining water quality. Without extra maintenance, artificial plants may nonetheless give aesthetic attractiveness to the tank/aquarium. Pick plants that are suitable for aquariums and the size of the tank.

- Driftwood and Rocks: Including driftwood and rocks may/can provide hiding places in the environment that are similar to the fish's natural habitat.

Make sure the materials are aquarium-safe and will not alter the chemistry of the tank water.

- Caves and ornaments: Platy fish like to hide out in locations where they can get away from stress in the tank. You may add shelter-giving structures like caves and tunnels as well as other aquarium-safe decorations to break up the visual area of the tank.

- Floating ornaments: Platy fish like to frolic close to the water's surface. Floating decorations may give interest and shade to their tank, such as floating plants or floating logs.

3. Safety Advice: - Steer clear of any objects with sharp edges or rough surfaces to protect platy fish's sensitive fins from cuts or injuries.

- Check to make sure the decorations are firmly in place and won't shift after, thereby hurting the fish or ruining the tank.

- If utilizing natural materials like rocks or driftwood, carefully clean and cure them to get rid of any extra tannins or other pollutants in it.

Keep in mind to organize the ornaments used so that the platy fish have access to free-swimming area while also offering them visual appeal and places to hide. A well-furnished aquarium not only improves its visual appeal but also offers your pet platy fish an exciting and cozy habitat.

2.4 Lighting and Heating Requirements

LIGTENING AND HEATING YOUR PLATY FISH TANK/AQUARIUM REQUIREMENTS;

1. **Lighting***:*

- *Moderate Intensity*: Platies don't have any particular lighting needs/requirements and may survive in environments with moderate illumination. Avoid illumination that is too harsh or too bright since it may/can stress people or promote excessive algae development in the tank.

- Photoperiod: Give your platy fish a consistent cycle of light and darkness to mimic the normal day and night cycle in nature. For a steady pattern, aim for 8~10 hours of daylight each day.

- Live Plants: If your tank contains live plants, take into account their lighting requirements as well. For their development, certain plants could need more light or a certain spectrum to flourish.

- Adjustable Lighting: Choose a lighting system that gives you the freedom/chance to alter the brightness or duration of the light as required. This will help you create the ambience you want in their tank.

2. Heating:

- Tropical Temperature Range: Platies are tropical fish, and they need a constant temperature between 72 and 82 degrees Fahrenheit (22 and 28 degrees Celsius) to survive/strive. In order to promote their general health and activity levels, it is essential to keep the water temperature within this given range.

- Aquarium Heater: To keep the aquarium at the proper temperature, use a dependable aquarium heater. Make sure the heater you choose has a built-in thermostat to precisely control the temperature itself and that it is the right size for your fish tank.

- Install a thermometer in the tank to frequently check the water's temperature. This enables you to be able to monitor the heater's performance and identify any irregularities that arises.

- Stability: keep the aquarium's temperature constant. The platy fish will be stressed or harmed by sudden changes in temperature body or by extreme variations.

- Room Temperature: Ensure that the aquarium is kept in a room with a consistent room temperature (not too cold not too hot). Extreme temperature in the room swings might have an impact on the tank's water temperature.

2.5 Cycling the Tank

Before introducing platy fish or any other species, the tank must be properly cycled to provide a stable and healthy habitat for them. Cycling is the process of establishing helpful bacteria in the fish aquarium that use the nitrogen cycle to change poisonous ammonia into less damaging compounds (nitrites and nitrates). An overview of how to cycle a platy tank is provided on this section of the book:

- Installation of the Tank:

Thoroughly rinse the substrate and decorations to get rid of any dust or dirt before using.

Add dechlorinated water to the tank. Use a water conditioner to treat the water to get rid of any heavy metals, chloramines, and chlorine.

- Add helpful Bacteria:

To jump-start the whole cycle process, add helpful bacteria. A commercial bacterial supplement made especially for aquarium cycling can do just fine to achieve this. For dose and application, follow according to the directions on the package.

- Check Water Parameters:

Test the water often to check the ammonia, nitrite, and nitrate levels.

Initially, when the bacteria colony grows, there can be an ammonia surge. As nitrite levels rise, ammonia levels should eventually decline.

- Be patient;

The cycle process often takes many weeks to achieve. Avoid adding fish before the tank has fully cycled and be patient.

- Ammonia and Nitrite Control:

Perform partial water changes regularly to dilute the poisons if ammonia or nitrite levels rise to unsafe levels and endanger your pet fish. Use water that has been well dechlorinated and treated with a water conditioner.

- Nitrate Control:

Nitrate concentrations will rise as the cycling process continues. To maintain nitrate levels below 40 ppm, do periodic partial water changes [25% of tank water}. By doing this, you can keep the water's quality high.

- Complete Cycle:

When ammonia and nitrite levels regularly read as zero 0, and nitrate levels are present but at a safe level for the fish, the cycling process is said to be complete.

You may/can progressively add your platy fish to the tank when it has finished cycling and the water conditions are steady to begin with

2.6 Adding Plants and Aquatic Life

Your surroundings will become more beautiful, have better air and water quality, and have a more balanced ecology if you add plants and aquatic life. Here are some pointers to get you all started if you're thinking about adding plants to your house, yard, or aquarium:

1. Adding Plants:

Check the lighting: Different plants demand different amounts of light.

Consider the lighting more in the area where you want to put plants and choose species that do well in low, medium, or high light levels.

2. Select appropriate plants: Take into account conditions like temperature, humidity, and upkeep needs of platies. Choose plants that will thrive well in your location and those you can properly maintain. You may choose between indoor and outdoor plants, or you can combine the two if you want.

3. Ensure good maintenance: Find out the exact requirements for the maintenance of the plants you choose to put, such as their demands,

schedule, and any unique requirements.

4. Arrange plants aesthetically: Plan the positioning and configuration of your plants to produce a beautiful and well-balanced show in the tank.

Adding Aquatic Life:

1. Create an Appropriate Habitat: Before introducing aquatic life in there, make sure the water is very suitable for the species you want to introduce. This entails maintaining ideal water quality, pH levels, and temperature. Do some research on the needs of the particular species you want to include in the tank.

2. Select species that get along: Not all aquatic animals can live together harmoniously in the same space. Some of them could have a propensity for violence or certain social demands. To make sure the species you intend to introduce can coexist successfully, research their compatibility with your existing fish.

3. Add fish gradually: When introducing fish to an aquarium do it slowly and gradually to give them time to adjust to their new surroundings. By doing so, stress is reduced and the ecology of the aquarium can adapt to the increasing bio-load included.

4. Give fish the right nutrition: Different fish species have different nutritional feed requirements. Make careful to give your fish a varied balanced diet that includes both commercial fish food and occasionally-added live or frozen species-specific meals.

5. Keep up with routine maintenance: Consistently check and maintain the quality of the tank water, including the temperature, pH, ammonia, nitrite, and nitrate levels. To keep your aquarium clean and a healthy habitat for your aquatic life, do routine water changes also.

CHAPTER 3. PLATY FISH CARE AND MAINTENANCE

3.1 Feeding Platy Fish

The omnivorous fish known as the platy fish (Xiphophorus maculatus) can consume a wide range of meals in their diet. Here is a list of usual foods eaten by platies as well as some items to stay away from:

What platies can eat

1. Premium flake food: A staple diet for platies that supplies all the necessary nutrients. Seek for flake

food designed especially for tropical fish.

2. Pellets: A variety of pellets, including those made specifically for platies, are available for tropical fish pellet. Pellets provide a well-rounded diet to your fish.

3. Live foods: Insect larvae, brine shrimp, and daphnia are among the live foods that platies like/enjoy. These may be cultivated at home or bought frozen commercially.

4. Frozen foods: Foods like brine shrimp, bloodworms, and daphnia that are frozen are very nutritious and easily ingested by platies.

5. Offer tiny pieces of blanched vegetables such as spinach, lettuce,

zucchini, and peas. These provide crucial vitamins and fiber added.

6. Algae wafers: Despite not being predominantly herbivorous, platies sometimes eat algae wafers, particularly if there are live plants present in the tank.

7. Spirulina-based foods: As a source of vegetable matter, platies benefit from periodic feedings of spirulina-based flakes or pellets.

Avoid these foods:

1. Processed human food: Steer clear of giving fish platies processed foods of any kind like bread, cereal, or anything else that isn't designed expressly for fish.

2. Never give raw meat to platies since it might contaminate the tank with parasites , disease or hazardous germs.

3. Spoiled or rotten food: To ensure high water quality, remove any uneaten food from the tank right away as seen.

Feeding Instructions:

Feed platies modest quantities two [2] to three [3] times daily. They should be given many tiny meals periodically rather than one big one since they have small stomachs.

2. Portion control: Only feed platies what they can finish in about 2-3 minutes. Overfeeding might result in

many health concerns and troubles with the water supply.

3. Variety: To provide a broad spectrum of nutrients to them, offer a diversified diet. Alternate between veggies, live or frozen meals, pellets, and flakes of food.

4. Observation: Keep an eye on the platies when they are being fed to make sure they all have access to food if you have more than one. It is important to keep an eye on your fish's behavior since certain species might be more aggressive than the other.

Every fish is different, and every of them has different nutritional requirements each. Depending on the behavior, look, and general health of your platies, adjust the feeding schedule used. Your fish will be healthier and more vibrant overall if you offer them a food that is well balanced and uses the right feeding techniques.

3.2 Water Quality and Maintenance

Keeping your platies' water in the best possible condition:

1. Water temperature: Platies, a kind of tropical fish, like water between 72°F and 82°F (22°C and 28°C) as recommended. Keep an eye on the temperature using a trustworthy

aquarium thermometer, and think about employing a heater to keep it going and steady.

2. pH Level: Platies like water with a pH between 7.0 and 8.0, which is somewhat more alkaline. Utilize a liquid test kit or test strips to regularly check the pH level of the water and, if required, make changes. To avoid stress and health problems, keep pH levels all steady.

3. Nitrite and ammonia levels: Nitrites and ammonia are hazardous elements to fish. To maintain steady levels of ammonia and nitrites, your aquarium has to establish a good nitrogen cycle. Beneficial microorganisms in the

aquarium filter transform any hazardous ammonia into the less dangerous nitrites and nitrates. Test the water's ammonia and nitrite levels on a regular basis and take the necessary precautions to maintain them at zero 0.

4. Nitrate Concentrations: Although nitrates are less poisonous than ammonia and nitrites, they may still be dangerous in large concentrations level. Nitrate levels may be controlled by performing regular water changes. Maintain nitrate concentrations at or below 40 ppm (parts per million). Every one to two weeks, carry out partial water changes of 20–30% to help keep the water quality high.

5. Filtration: To eliminate trash, surplus water waste, and pollutants from the water, an effective aquarium filter is required. Choose a filter that is appropriate for the size of your aquarium and adhere to the care recommendations provided by the manufacturer of the product used. To guarantee effective filtration, replace or regularly clean the filter mediums fixed.

6. Water Changes: Changing the water on a regular basis is very essential to preserving water quality. As previously noted, execute 20–30% partial water changes every one to two weeks. To avoid it decaying and

impairing water quality, siphon off any trash or debris from the ground during regular water changes.

7. Chlorine and Chloramines: Fish are harmed by chlorine and chloramines, which are often present in tap water. Before introducing tap water to your aquarium during water changes, neutralize these toxins in it with a water conditioner or dechlorinator. For the right dose, according to the conditioner's directions.

8. Monitoring: Use the proper test kits to routinely check the water parameters. This will solely assist you

in early problem detection and rapid remedial action.

Keep in mind that maintaining steady and ideal water quality is a never-ending task. Your platy fish will live in a healthy environment with regular testing, monitoring, and the right management practices.

3.3 Tank Mates and Compatibility

Platy fish get along well with a variety of tank mates since they are often knwon calm and social. When choosing tank mates for your platies, take into account elements like size, temperament, and water conditions of each. These fish are good tank mates for platy fish recommended:

1. Guppies (Poecilia reticulata): Guppies are very good tank mates for platies because of their comparable care needs and calm disposition. In the same tank, both species may live in peace and harmony.

2. Swordtails (Xiphophorus hellerii): Swordtails and platies share a similar life cycle and care needs. They get along nicely with platies and are also calm fish.

3. Tetras: A wide variety of tetra species, including neon tetras (Paracheirodon innesi) and black skirt tetras (Gymnocorymbus ternetzi), may/can make good tank mates for platies. Make sure the tetras are little for the space and peaceful.

4. Corydoras catfish: Peaceful bottom-dwelling fish that get along with platies include corydoras catfish like the bronze cory (Corydoras aeneus). They scavenge for food to keep the tank clean and less of un eaten food.

5. Harlequin Rasboras (Trigonostigma heteromorpha): These little, calm fish get along well with platies and give the aquarium some color and life of its

own. They like water with comparable characteristics with platy.

6. Mollies (Poecilia sphenops): Mollies are normally very calm and have comparable care needs as platies. In the same tank, they may live in harmony. Avoid maintaining male mollies with lengthy finnage, however, since they might mistakenly think they are platies and startle them.

7. Livebearers in general: Platies are a member of the Poeciliidae family, which also includes mollies, guppies, and swordtail fish. These species often get along nicely with one another and are all platy compatible.

Think about the size of your tank while choosing your tank mates. Make sure it is big enough to hold the selected species you want to add, enabling room for swimming and reducing territorial disputes between them.

Avoid fish that are aggressive or fin-nipping since doing so might cause stress or hurt platies. Fish like aggressive cichlids, barbs, and bigger aggressive species should be avoided as platy tank mates.

Always keep an eye on how various species get along in your aquarium and be ready to make changes if any aggressiveness or compatibility problems starts to occur. Stress and hostility among tank mates may be decreased by offering plenty of hiding spots and a lush habitat.

Others in the tank

Potential tank mates for platy fish include the following:

- First guppies
- Swordtails, 2.
- Tetras (including neon tetras and black skirt tetras),
- Corydoras catfish,
- Harlequin rasboras,
- Mollies are also included.
- Angelfish 7.

- Gouramis 8.
- 9. Cherry barbs,
- 10. Rainbowfish,
- and 11. Danios
- Minnows from the White Cloud Mountains
- Otocinclus catfish 13.
- Ghost shrimp 14.
- 15. snails, particularly nerite or mystery snails

Overall, platies may/can happily cohabit with a variety of community fish in a well-maintained aquarium with careful thought and sufficient stocking in their tank.

3.4 Disease Prevention and Treatment

Although platy fish are mostly resilient, several illnesses may still affect them. The following list of prevalent ailments that might affect your platies includes both preventative and treatment options:

1. Prevention of Ich (White Spot fish Disease): Maintain high water quality, prevent abrupt temperature changes, and reduce any form of stress. Before adding additional fish to the main tank, quarantine them.

Treatment: The temperature should be raised to around 82°F (28°C), and the whole tank should be treated with an ich disease medicine that contains malachite green or a mixture of malachite green and formalin. For dose and duration, abide by the directions on the prescription packaging of the product.

2. Prevention of Fin Rot: Keep the water in very good condition and clean. To promote excellent general health, avoid overcrowding and provide a well-balanced diet.

Treatment: Consistent water changes will improve the quality of the water. Utilize a broad-spectrum antibiotic created especially for the treatment of fin rot disease. For dose and duration, abide by the directions on the prescription packaging and consult a veterinarian if the problem becomes way worse.

3. Fungal Illnesses

Prevention: Keep the water in top quality condition, protect the fish from harm, and empty the tank of any decomposing organic materials in it.

Use antifungal drugs or therapies designed especially for fish as a kind of therapy. For dose and duration, abide by the directions on the prescription packaging. As advised by a veterinarian, raise the quality of the water and think about adding aquarium base salt (sodium chloride).

4. Swimbladder Conditions:

Prevention: Avoid overfeeding and provide a balanced diet. To achieve a balanced diet, provide a range of foods for your fish.

Treatment: To ease constipation, provide a little quantity of high-fiber meals, such as boiled peas with the skin peeled/removed. Adapt the diet to include items that are simple to digest. A veterinarian/doctor should be consulted if the issue or problem continues.

5. To prevent velvet disease, keep the water in top condition, stay away from irritants, and quarantine any new fish before putting them in the main tank.

Treatment: Raise the temperature to around 82°F (28°C), then use a treatment made especially for treating velvet to sanitize the whole fish tank. For dose and duration, abide by the directions on the prescription packaging.

6. Prevention for Columnaris (Mouth Fungus): Maintain immaculate water quality, abstain from congestion, and maintain a stress-free fish atmosphere. Use drugs created especially for columnaris as a type of treatment for them. For dose and duration, abide by the directions on the prescription packaging of the drug. Enhance the quality of the water and think about

adding aquarium salt as advised by a veterinarian.

Keep in mind that sustaining the health of your platy fish depends on appropriate prevention and early detection of any disease.

3.5 Breeding and Rearing Fry

Platypus breeding may be a satisfying endeavor to their owners. The following recommendations are for breeding platies and raising their fry:

Sexing: Differentiate between male and female platies before trying to breeding them. While females have a rounded anal fin, males have an extended and pointed gonopodium, a modified anal fin.

Breeding Tank: Construct an additional different breeding tank or use a breeding net within the primary tank. The aquarium must to contain a heater to keep the temperature constant at 77–80°F (25–27°C), plants for cover, and a soft filtration system planted.

Pairing: Add one or two females to the breeding tank for every one male. It's crucial to allow women enough room to get away from men's attention and avoid any stress.

Conditioning: Make sure the men and females are fed properly with varies of meals and in excellent health before breeding process. Give your pet a healthy diet consisting of premium flakes, pellets, live, or frozen meals, and every so often, give them little portions of live plants or vegetables to their diet.

Mating and Gestation: During mating, the male platy will place his gonopodium into the vent of the female to fertilize her. The female will then store the sperm internally after mating, allowing her to have numerous broods from a single union. Platy fish normally have a gestation period of 4-6 weeks after.

After the female has given birth, remove her from the breeding tank to stop her from eating up the fry.

 1. Separate the Fry. Because the fry are so little and delicate, it's critical to offer a secure environment for their development so as to keep them.

2. Nursery Tank: To raise the fry, either set up a separate nursery tank for them or utilize a breeding net within

the main tank. To offer mild filtering, use a sponge filter or an air-driven filter for it.

3. Feed the fry with liquid fry specific food, powdered fry food, or specialty fry food. These are better suited to their little lips since they are smaller in size. To make sure they get enough food, give them modest, frequent feedings portions.

4. Water Quality: Keep the nursery tank's water in top condition and maintain the environment clean and reduce stress on the fry, do routine water changes.

5. Gradual Growth: Introduce larger food sources, such as newly hatched brine shrimp, micro worms, or finely crushed flakes, as the fry become bigger and grows. As the fry grow, progressively enlarge the food.

6. Monitoring and Separation: Keep an eye on the fry's growth and slow development. Some fry may develop more vivid colors or unique patterns as they mature over time. To avoid interbreeding while selecting breeding for a certain feature, divide the fry with the desired traits into different tanks.

7. Tank Size: As the fry mature, you may need to move them to tanks with

more space as their populations and sizes expands with them.

3.6 Tips for Handling and Acclimating Platy Fish

Reduce stress and facilitate a seamless transition for platy fish while handling and acclimating them to their new surroundings. Here are some pointers for taking care of and adjusting to platy fish:

1. Usage a net: Use a soft mesh net made exclusively for aquarium usage for catching or transferring your platy fish. To avoid hurting or harming their fragile scales, stay away from using

your hands or other sharp items with them.

2. Be Gentle: Treat platy fish gently and steer clear of applying too much pressure or squeezing them. They have really sensitive bodies and are often hurt when handled carelessly.

3. Damp Hands: If handling platy fish with your hands is necessary, make sure they are well damp first. Wet hands reduce the amount of time that their body's natural barrier against any illness, the slime coat, is lost.

Getting Used to Platy Fish

1. Floating technique: Use the floating technique to acclimate new platy fish

in the tank when taking them home from the pet shop or placing them in a new aquarium. For roughly 14-20 minutes, float the sealed bag holding the fish in the tank. Consequently, the water within the bag may gradually warm up to the tank temperature adaptable.

2. Drip technique: You may utilize the drip acclimation technique for platy fish that are more fragile or sensitive. Put the fish in a container, then gradually add aquarium water to the container used over time in little quantities. As a result, the water's temperature, pH, and chemical make-

up progressively normalize, lowering the stress on the pet fish.

3. Water Parameter Match: It's crucial to match the water parameters of the tank closely that platy fish are moving into while acclimating them. This covers the following: temperature, pH value, and water hardness. To verify adequate water parameters in the aquarium and the quarantine or shipping bag, use a dependable water testing kit/instrument.

4. Steer clear of unexpected changes in water conditions since platy fish are sensitive to them. When acclimating, stay away from direct air contact,

sudden temperature fluctuations or change, and significant changes in the water's properties.

5. Release Fish Carefully: After they've become used to you, use a net to release the fish slowly into the aquarium. As the water from the shipping bag might contain toxins or diseases, avoid adding it to the main aquarium.

6. Decrease Lighting: To assist the fish in acclimating to their new environment and lessen any stress, decrease the aquarium lights after acclimation or provide proper hiding places.

By paying attention to these suggestions, you may make your platy fish feel less anxious and have an easy time acclimating to their new surroundings.

CHAPTER 4.

UNDERSTANDING PLATY FISH BEHAVIOR

4.1 Social Structure and Behavior Patterns

Platies are known as schooling fish, which means they like being with others rather than being all alone. They will act more naturally and feel more confident if you keep them in groups of at least five or more fish.

Pecking Order and Hierarchy: A pecking order or hierarchy may form among a platy population. Fish who are dominant may assert their dominance and act in a territorial manner. To reduce violence among tank mates, it's crucial to give plenty of hiding spots and space for them.

Platies often have a tranquil disposition and get along well with other peaceful neighborhood fish. They don't usually act aggressively until it's too crowded or stressed, there aren't enough hiding places, or there isn't enough territory for each.

Male platies are renowned for their wooing displays/behaviors to entice females during mating and courtship. They flaunt their flared fins, exhibit proper vivid colors, and pursue females. The male platy will choose a partner, and the female will be fertilized by the male using his gonopodium (a modified anal fin).

Platies are live bearers fishes, which means that they give birth to live, fully grown fry (newborn) rather than laying eggs for males to fertilize. The female will show signs of pregnancy after mating by developing a gravid patch next to her anal fin. Usually, the gestational period lasts 3-6 weeks.

Platies are vigorous swimmers that explore the whole aquarium's levels. It is best to provide a well-planted environment with wide swimming places since they like to swim among plants and decorations.

Platies are typically calm and get along with a wide range of neighborhood fish, including other livebearers like guppies and mollies. They get along with tranquil rasboras, smaller tetras, and bottom-dwelling fish like corydoras catfish.

Platies participate socially within their group, showing off behaviors like schooling, swimming in timed patterns, and even flashing their fins. You may create a setting that supports the platy fish's wellbeing and innate preferences by observing and comprehending their social activities.

4.2 Communication and Interactions

The methods that platy fish engage and communicate with one another vary. The following are some facets of their interactional and communicative behaviors discussed in this section of the guide:

Visual Displays: Platies communicate by using visual displays. During courting displays, male platies often show vivid colors and expanded fins to entice their females. As a territorial or dominance show, they may also flare their fins or act aggressively toward other males.

Body Language: Platies communicate with one another via their bodies. They exhibit submissive behavior by bending their bodies, lowering their fins, or becoming pallid.

Schooling Behavior: Platies are sociable schooling fish that engage well with one another. They maintain close closeness to the other swimmers in the school as they swim in synchronized patterns together. Their education gives them a feeling of safety, security and enables them to move in unison.

Interactions with Fry: Female platies treat their fry with maternal affection. Young fry may/can get protection and guidance from them, and they learn to follow their mother for protection. Understanding the social dynamics and parental behavior of platy fish should be gained by observing this connection.

Platies respond to their surroundings by exhibiting a variety of behaviors. They could inspect new items to the tank, swim amid plants or decorations, or just explore their environment in the tank. Behavior and social relations may vary in response to changes in the water environment or the addition of new tank mates.

Fish keepers design an environment that supports platy fish's natural behaviors and social dynamics by having an understanding of these specific communication and interaction activities they exhibit. The general well-being of platies is influenced by offering a well-organized tank, selecting suitable tank mates, and seeing to it that their social requirements are all satisfied.

4.3 Aggression and Conflict Resolution

A pecking order or hierarchy may develop among platies in a group because of aggression and dominance. Dominant people establish their dominance by acting aggressively or in a territorial manner. This can include pursuing or biting at inferior fishes in the tank. It reduces hostility among tank mates to provide plenty of hiding spots and room in the tank for them.

4.4 Breeding Behavior and Reproduction

Male platies engage in courting and mating actions to entice females. This behavior include running after the female, flashing bright colors at her, and doing fin displays. Females have the option of choosing a partner, and effective wooing results in internal fertilization of her eggs.

CHAPTER 5.
EXPLORING PLATY
FISH VARIETIES

5.1 Common Varieties: Colorful and Classic

1. Mickey Mouse Platy: This species gets its name from the black patterns on its tail, which resemble the outline of the popular Mickey Mouse. The body colors is often a vivid red or orange hue. The form and intensity of the black marks might change.

2. Wagtail Platy: Wagtail platies feature a characteristic tail fin with a black or dark-hued like crescent-

shaped pattern. Their bodies are often colored in colors of red, orange, or yellow. They get their name from the tail, which has the appearance of a wagging tail shown.

3. The tuxedo platy has a body that is mostly dark in color—*usually black*—with brightly colorful spots on its fins and overall body. The contrast between the dark base color and the vivid spots gives the coloring pattern the appearance of a tuxedo.

4. Sunset Platy: Sunset platies are distinguished by their spectacular colour and brilliant hues. They often exhibit a mixture of orange, red, and

yellow tones that resemble a stunning sunset view. Males' colors may seem more vibrant during courting displays.

5. Red Platy: The body, fins, and tail of red platies are all uniformly and intensely red in color. This cultivar is well-liked for its striking look.

6. Variatus platies are available in a variety of hues, including red, orange, yellow, blue, and green. They often have elaborate patterns and vibrant color combinations, which give the aquarium more visual appeal to look .

7. Albino platy: Lacking pigmentation, albino platies have a creamy, creamy-white like body and pink or red eyes.

When housed alongside other fish that have vibrant colors, their distinct look may provide a stunning contrast with other fish colors.

5.2 Rare and Exotic Platy Fish

While there are a few number of popular platy fish variations, there are also several uncommon and exotic kinds that are less often seen in the aquarium trade.

1. The Panda platy is an uncommon species with a stunning black and white color. Typically, the body is white or cream with black dots on it or

patches that resemble a panda's coloring. Because of its distinctive and eye-catching look, it is widely sought after in the market.

2. Metallic platy: Due to the metallic pigments in their scales, metallic platies have a glossy and reflective look. They may be found in a variety of hues, including metallic blue, silver, and gold, which gives the aquarium a refined feel or appearance.

3. The unique species known as the "Marigold platy" has a vivid yellow or gold color all over its body. Its vivid hue may mimic the marigold known flower's bright petals.

4. Rainbow platy: This species of platy displays a variety of hues, often in tones of red, orange, yellow, blue, and green. They are quite prized for their brilliant and iridescent colour, which may make for an eye-catching aquarium display.

5. Calico Platy: Calico platies have patches of black, orange, red, yellow, and white along with other colors and patterns. The final result has a lovely mosaic-like design that is reminiscent of certain animals' calico pattern.

It is important to note that depending on the location and local breeders or suppliers, the availability of these uncommon and exotic platy fish species may vary.

5.3 Selective Breeding and Genetic Considerations

Selective breeding is a technique used to develop desirable qualities in a particular species or variation by deliberately selecting certain traits of fishes and passing them down through subsequent generations. Selective breeding has been crucial in creating the vast variety of hues, patterns, and fin shapes seen in the numerous platy pet fish types that are now on the market for the platy fish (Xiphophorus maculatus).

Here are some genetic factors and breeding strategies for platy fish:

1. Phenotype Selection: Breeders choose individuals with certain physical characteristics they like, or phenotypes, for breeding, such as vivid colors, distinctive body patterns, or unusual fin forms. Breeders try to improve and maintain desirable qualities in succeeding generations by choosing and mating fish with such traits.

2. Line breeding: To reinforce and fine-tune desired qualities, fish from the same lineage or closely related individuals are bred together. This method helps in ensuring that the desired traits in the offspring show up consistently and predictably, as you want.

3. Crossbreeding: To introduce novel genetic fusions and produce hybrid progeny, crossbreeding entails breeding fish from several different strains or kinds. Unique and new color patterns or fin forms that may not be present in the parent kinds can be produced using this known procedure.

4. Inbreeding and Outbreeding: Inbreeding refers to the mating of individuals who are closely related, such as siblings or parent-child pairings. Although it bears the risk of collecting genetic features that are not wanted, it may assist correct beneficial ones. On the other side, outbreeding includes breeding fish from distantly related or unrelated lines to increase genetic diversity and lower the danger of any genetic problems brought on by inbreeding.

5. Genetic Health: The general health and welfare of the fish should come first in selective breeding process. Breeders should carefully choose and

monitor breeding stock in order to reduce genetic flaws or susceptibility to certain prone illnesses.

6. Patience and Observation: Selective breeding calls for endurance and an acute eye for seeing minute changes and advancements in the desired qualities over several generations. Breeders must carefully monitor and evaluate the progeny, choosing the most promising ones for further breeding practices.

Ethical breeding methods should put the wellbeing of the fish first and work to preserve genetic variation. Reduced genetic diversity and related health problems might result from inbreeding or strong selection for certain body features. Breeders should also make sure that the fish used in the breeding process have the proper habitat, nourishment, and care given.

The numerous and aesthetically attractive platy fish types we see today have mostly been the result of selective breeding practice. The need of maintaining a balanced strategy that takes into account the fish's long-term genetic health as well as its visual appeal cannot be overstated.

CHAPTER 6;
ADVANCED PLATY
FISH KEEPING

6.1 Tank Size and Population Management

For the wellbeing and general health of platy fish (Xiphophorus maculatus), tank size and population control in the tank are crucial considerations. Following are some recommendations for population control and tank size:

1. Tank Size:

As a general rule, a small group of platies should have a tank that is at least 10 gallons (37-38 liters) in size. However, bigger tanks are usually recommended since they provide the fish greater stability and swimming room.

2. Take into Account the Amount of Fish: The quantity of platies you may maintain in a tank relies on the size of the tank you have and the particular kind of platy. As a starting point, think about giving each adult platy at least 2 gallons (7.5 liters) of water. This makes it easier for them to swim and lessens competition for resources in the aquarium.

3. Tank size: Take into account both the capacity and the size of the tank. Since platies are quite energetic

swimmers, a tank with a minimum length of 24 inches (60 cm) offers greater area for horizontal swimming.

4. Population Control:

Appropriate Group Size: Because platies are sociable fish, it is best to keep them in groups of about five or more. By giving them a group, you enable them to engage in their natural learning behaviors and lessen stress.

5. Gender Ratio:

It's important to maintain a balanced gender ratio in your tank. To spread out the male's attention and lessen the likelihood of excessive chasing or hostility toward a single female in it, it is advised to have at least two females for every male in the fish tank.

6. Take into mind your tank mates: When deciding how many fish to keep in your aquarium, consider how well platies get along with different fish species you want in there. To reduce stress and hostility, avoid overcrowding and make sure that the tank mates have comparable care needs and personalities.

4. Refrain from overstocking. Overstocking may result in frequent contaminated water, stress, and a

higher risk of getting illness. For the quantity of fish in the tank, it's essential to offer enough room and filtration power for this. Optimal conditions are ensured by frequent water testing and maintenance procedures followed.

5. Growth Factors: Keep in mind that platies may reproduce very fast and that a small population of platies can expand into a bigger one very soon. If you don't want a lot of fry, segregate the sexes or think about having only one gender in each tank to avoid accidental breeding.

6.2 Breeding Methods, Genetics, and How-to-Breed

It might be satisfying to breed platy fish (Xiphophorus maculatus). The following breeding methods and genetic factors should be taken into account while breeding your platy fish:

1. Choosing Breeding Stock:
- Select mature, well healthy adult platies with appealing characteristics like vivid colors, fin forms, or patterns.
  - Seek for people who display all the traits that you wish to pass on to their progeny.

2. Breeding Tank Setup: Use a breeding net within the main tank or set up a separate breeding tank.

- Give the woman someplace to hide from the man's approaches, such as plants or decorations to avoid stress.

- Maintain water conditions that are well suitable for platies, including the pH and temperature.

3. Pairing and Courtship:

- In the breeding tank, introduce one or more females to a male.

- To entice the female, the male will engage in courting activities such chasing, fin flaring, and vivid body color displays.

- The female will choose a partner, and the male will use his gonopodium to fertilize her once.

4. Spawning and Gestation: Following a fruitful mating, the female will internally store the male's sperm.
   - She will go through gestation, which normally lasts 3-6 weeks.
   - Keep an eye out for the gravid spot, which is a darkening patch close to the female's anal fin and signifies pregnancy in them.

5. Fry Care and Rearing: - To stop the female from consuming the fry she birth after giving birth, remove her from the breeding fish tank.

- Provide a separate nursery tank or house the fry in a breeding net.

- Feed the fry powdered flakes or specialist fry food made for their tiny platy lips.

- Ensure the right water conditions and keep an eye on their gradual development.

1. Genetic considerations: Selected breeding: Selected breeding involves choosing individuals with desirable qualities and stabilizing those traits in later generations made.

2. Line breeding and outcrossing: Outcrossing provides genetic variation by mating platies that are unrelated or just distantly related, while line

breeding involves pairing closely related individuals to fix desirable features they havel.

3. Genetic Wellness: Limit your inbreeding as much as possible to lower your chance of any forming genetic disorders. To encourage healthy progeny, keep an eye on and maintain the breeding stock's general genetic health.

4. Observing and Choosing Offspring: To further improve desired qualities, observe the offspring for desirable attributes and choose the most promising individuals out of them for further breeding.

Remember that fish welfare and health come first in appropriate breeding procedures. Throughout the breeding phase, it's critical to provide the right care, keep an eye on the water quality, and maintain ideal tank conditions.

6.3 Health Concerns and Treatments

1. Ich (White Spot fish Disease): Symptoms include white patches on the fish body and fins that flash when they come into contact with items.

- Treatments The temperature should be raised to around 82°F (28°C), and the whole tank should be treated with an ich medicine that contains malachite green or a mixture of malachite green and formalin before affecting others. For dose and duration, abide by the directions on the prescription packaging.

2. Fin Rot: - Signs and symptoms include fraying, discolouration of body, and inflammation of the fins.

- Solutions: Increase water quality by doing routine water changes daily. Utilize a broad-spectrum antibiotic created especially for the treatment of fin rot in fishes. For dose and duration, abide by the directions on the prescription packaging. Make sure the atmosphere in the tank is stress-free and clean.

3. Symptoms of fungal infections in them include white or gray growths on the body, fins, or mouth.

- Treatments Use antifungal drugs or treatments designed especially for fish illness like this. For dose and duration, abide by the directions on the prescription packaging. Enhance the quality of the water and think about adding aquarium salt as advised by a veterinarian or aquarist.

4. Swim bladder disorders: - Symptoms include trouble swimming

straight, floating at the top/surface, or sinking to the bottom.

- Treatments to ease constipation, provide a little quantity of more high-fiber meals, such as boiled peas with the skin removed. Adapt the diet to include items that are simple to digest.

5. Symptoms of parasitic infections include scratching against things in the tank and the presence of visible parasites on the body or fins.

- Treatment options: Determine which parasites need to be treated and use the relevant drugs or treatments given by your vet. To get the right diagnosis and care, see a veterinarian.

Symptoms of bacterial infections include open sores, ulcers, redness in body, inflammation, lethargic behavior or trait, and appetite loss.

Use antibiotics made particularly for fish and according to the dose and administration guidelines listed on the prescription packaging. Keep the water in top good condition and create a calm atmosphere.

7. Lethargy, lack of appetite, fast breathing, and fin degeneration are all the signs of poor water quality.

- Treatments To keep your water quality at its best, replace the water very often. Keep an eye on the pH, nitrate, nitrite, and ammonia levels of the water. Make sure there is enough filtration going on and provide the fish a clean habitat.

It's crucial to remember that the best way to get the right diagnosis and treatment is with the help of a/your veterinarian or an expert fish keeper. When dealing with any health difficulties, keep a tight eye on the fish behavior, keep the environment steady and clean, and swiftly seek expert guidance if necessary. The best way to reduce the likelihood of platy fish developing any health issues is via prevention through good health care and routine maintenance.

6.4 Aquascaping and Platy Fish Tank Design

The skill of planning and arranging aquatic plants, rocks, driftwood, and other objects in a fish tank to produce an attractive and realistic-looking underwater environment is known as the term *aquascaping*. The common freshwater aquarium fish known as platy fish, moonfish or platies, are bright, simple to care for fishes, and ideal for aquascaping arrangements.

The following things should be checked while creating an aquascape for a platy fish tank:

1. The size of the tank is very important because, while being little fish, platies still require room to swim and explore around. For a small group of platies, a tank with a minimum capacity of 10 gallons is advised.

2. Substrate: Pick a substrate that complements the design of your aquascape you chose. Sand, gravel, or specialty aquatic plant substrates are available as options to try. Dark substrates might assist bring out your platy fish's vivid colors.

3. Aquatic plants: A vital element of aquascaping are live tank plants. They provide the water natural hiding

places, oxygenate the tank water, and support water quality maintenance. Consider utilizing a range of plant species in there, such as dwarf hairgrass as carpeting, anubias, java fern, and Vallisneria for the backdrop and Amazon swords and Vallisneria for the foreground and midground, respectively.

4. Hardscape: Include hardscape components, like as pebbles and driftwood, to offer aesthetic [beauty] interest and produce fish-friendly hiding places. Make sure the rocks you choose are aquarium-safe and won't change the water's chemistry over time. Additionally, driftwood may

provide as a surface for the development of advantageous algae, which the platies may use as food source.

5. Illumination and CO2: Give the plants in your aquascape the proper illumination. For the majority of platy fish tanks out there, low to moderate illumination is usually enough for them. If you choose high-light plants, think about supplementing with CO_2 to encourage strong and firm plant development.

6. Water characteristics: Platies are tolerant fish that may live in a variety of water settings. But it's crucial to

keep the water's characteristics steady. Maintain a pH range of 7.0~8.2 and a temperature range of 72~82°F (22~28°C) for the water. A healthy habitat for the fish and plants may be quite ensured with regular water testing and the right filtration.

7. Fish compatibility: Platies are calm fish and get along well with different types of neighborhood fish [tank mates]. The fish you pick to keep alongside platies should not be aggressive or prone to any nibble at the platies' fins, and they should also have comparable water parameter needs.

To keep the tank healthy and aesthetically pleasing, don't forget to periodically maintain and clean your aquascape used by pruning plants, cleaning any debris, and making daily water changes. Feel free to explore and modify the design as you see fit to create a lovely environment for your platy fish since aquascaping is an imaginative and satisfying pastime for any platy owner to go about in.

CHAPTER 7;
FREQUENTLY ASKED QUESTIONS (FAQS)

7.1 General Question

The following are some typical queries concerning platy fish:

What exactly are platy fish?

Small, calm, and vibrant platy fish (Xiphophorus maculatus), which are endemic to Central America, are freshwater kmown fish. They are well-liked by aquarium hobbyists because of their vivid colors, simplicity of maintenance, and lively personalities.

2. How do platy fish appear?

Platies are available in a wide range of hues and body designs. Their bodies are normally rounder, and their snouts are all pointy. The colour may be a variety of these hues alone or in combinations, such as solid red, orange, yellow, or blue type. Some platies also have patterns on their body or fins, such as dark or black striped marks.

What size aquarium is best for platy fish?

Platies may be maintained in aquariums as little as 10 gallons since they are very tiny fish. However, if you want to retain a small group of platies together or include other fish species, a bigger tank, such as one that is 20 gallons long or greater, is well advised.

What water characteristics are ideal for platy fish?

Platies are tolerant fish that can live in a variety of aquatic environments given. Maintain a pH range of 7.0~8.2 and a water temperature of 72~82°F (22~28°C). They can tolerate a range of water hardness levels but prefer fairly hard water more.

How many platy fish may be maintained in close proximity?

Because they are sociable fish, platies need to be maintained in groups of at least three [3] to five [5]. They may/can reproduce swiftly because they are livebearers, which means they give birth to fry while still alive rather than eggs. If you don't want the platy population to become out of hand, it's crucial to think about the tank size and population control methods before trying.

What do platy fish consume?

Platies eat a variety of things(food) and are omnivores. High-quality flake or pellet feeds made for tropical fish will be easily consumed by them. Additionally, it is advantageous to include tiny live or frozen meals to their diet once in a while, such as brine shrimp, daphnia, or bloodworms. They will also eat the aquarium's algae and other plant material.

Can platy fish coexist peacefully with other fish species?

Platies may be maintained alongside other peaceful community fish species including tetras, guppies, mollies, and swordtails since they are typically known peaceful. Avoid keeping them with fish that are shown aggressive or fin-nipping as this might stress the platies and perhaps injure them.

How can male and female platy fish be distinguished?

Male platies are way more colorful and smaller than females. The gonopodium, or modified anal fin, on males is long and thin. The anal fin of females is typically fan-shaped looking. On occasion, pregnant female platies may display the gravid spot, a dark seen area close to the belly.

Are platy fish easy to breed?

Yes, platy fish reproduce a lot. They give birth to live fry because they are livebearers. In the absence of separation or population management in the tank, male and female platies kept together are very prone to breed. Giving birth to fry may assist prevent them from being eaten by other fish by providing more hiding places like thick foliage or breeding traps.

The lifespan of platy fish.

A platy fish may survive for three-five (3-5) years with the right care. Their lifetime may be increased by providing a clean tank environment, a proper balanced food, and reducing stressors.

7.2 Tank Configuration and Upkeep

The following are some often asked questions concerning the construction and maintenance of platy fish tanks:

How should a platy fish tank be set up?

- Rinse the tank first, then add an appropriate substrate in it.

- To preserve the purity of the water, install a filter system for filtration.

- Include extras like real plants, driftwood, and pebbles in it.

- Before introducing fish, fill the tank with well conditioned water and give it time to cycle up.

- Keep an eye on the water's characteristics and make any modifications. needed

.How often should I clean my tank of platy fish?

- Every 1-2 weeks, do routine maintenance, which should include partial water changes (around 25-30% of the tank's content).

- When changing the water, use a siphon to remove any trash and debris from the substrate.

- Regularly clean the filter media to avoid blockage and maintain effective filtering in the tank.

What ought my platy fish to eat?

- Provide a well-balanced diet made up of premium flake or pellet meals made for tropical freshwater fish.

- Occasionally give them live or frozen things like brine shrimp, daphnia, or bloodworms to supplement their diet/feeding.

- Including some vegetable stuff, such as blanched spinach or flakes made of spirulina, is also advantageous to them.

How can I make sure the water conditions are ideal for my platy fish?

- Conduct routine tests on the water's temperature, pH, ammonia, nitrite, and nitrate levels daily.

- Maintain the pH level between 7.0 and 8.2, and the water temperature between 72 and 82 °F (22 and 28 °C).

- To get heavy metals, chlorine, and chloramines out of tap water, use a dependable water conditioner for this.

- To eliminate contaminants, make sure the filtering is sufficient and think about adding activated carbon or other chemical filter media inside.

Are platy fish capable of withstanding varying water hardness levels?

- Platies are tolerant of a variety of water hardness levels and are quite adaptive.

- Although they may adapt to softer or harsher water conditions, they typically favor somewhat more of hard water.

- Keep the water's characteristics steady to prevent abrupt changes that can stress the pet fish.

Do I need to illuminate the tank where my platy fish are kept?

If you have live plants in your tank, lighting is quite crucial.

- Based on the requirements of your plants, choose the right aquarium lighting.

- To promote wholesome plant development, allow for an 8~10 hour period of light each day.

How can I add fresh platy fish to the aquarium?

- Float the bag in the tank for 15 to about 20 minutes to acclimate new fish to the tank's temperature.

- Open the bag and gradually pour tank water to it in little volumes.

- After acclimatization, cautiously release the fish into the main tank to prevent abrupt changes in the water's conditions.

Can I maintain other kinds of fish beside platies?

- Platies may cohabit with other peaceful community fish species since they are typically calm and social fish.

- Keep your distance from aggressive or fin-nipping fish that could annoy or worry/stress the platies.

- Do your homework on the compatibility and unique needs of the fish species you want to keep together with them.

Remember that these are just basic recommendations, and it's crucial to learn about the particular requirements of platy fish as well as any additional fish or plants you want to include in your aquarium.

7.3 Breeding platy fish without a doubt!

The following are some typical queries concerning platy fish breeding:

\How do platy fish reproduce?

- Platies are livebearers, which means they don't lay eggs but instead give birth to live fry (new born).

- A unique anal fin on the male platy termed a gonopodium is employed for internal fertilization.

- When a man is ready to procreate, he will pursue the female and engage in courtship behavior themselves.

- The male will fertilize the eggs internally by transferring sperm to the female via his gonopodium.

2. How can I determine when my platy fish are mature enough to reproduce?

- When a female platy fish is pregnant, a gravid spot, a dark area around the belly, will definitely appear.

- As the female gets closer to giving birth, the gravid spot becomes more and more noticeable.

- During breeding season, males may engage in greater pursuing activity and display more vivid colors.

3. What equipment do I need to set up for platy fish breeding?

- To safeguard young fry, the aquarium should have plenty of hiding spots placed, such as thick foliage or breeding traps.

To increase the likelihood that fry will survive, keep the pregnant mother fish apart from other fish in the tank.

- Maintain an aquarium environment that is stable and has the proper water placed conditions.

4. How long does a platy fish take to mature?

- Although it might quite vary, the gestation time for platy fish is normally between 27 and 30 days.

- Since female platies may store sperm for subsequent fertilization, they can produce numerous batches of fry from just a single mating.

5. Do platy fish consume their own young?

- Especially in a communal tank with other fish, adult platies may devour their own fry once born. It is advised to offer hiding places for fry safety where they may find cover, such as thick foliage or breeding traps, to increase fry survival rates in there.

6. How should I handle platy fry?

It's crucial to provide the fry an appropriate habitat after they are born.

- For the first several weeks, feed the fry all crushed or powdered fish meal, specialist fry diet, or infusoria.

- Change the water often to keep it in excellent condition for the developing born fry.

- As they develop, they add bigger items like young brine shrimp or powdered flakes to their feed schedule.

7. How quickly do platy fry develop?

Fish called platies grow quite quickly. They may grow to a size of around 1 inch (2.5 cm) in a few months after birth with the right care and nourishment.

8. Is it possible to breed platy fish in a shared tank?

- It is feasible to breed platy fish in a communal tank, but the chances of the fry surviving may/can be reduced.

- The fry may be eaten by other fish, including mature platies of their kind.

- Consider establishing a separate breeding tank or using breeding traps in the communal tank to increase your fry survival.

7.4 Disease and Health Management

Here are some often asked queries about the treatment of illnesses in platy fish:

How can I maintain the health of my platy fish?

- Keep your aquarium very clean and in good condition by using correct filtration and regular water changes.

- Offer a well-balanced diet that includes premium fish food and sporadic additions of live or frozen items.

- Maintain consistent water conditions that fall within the platy fish-friendly range.

- Prevent overcrowding in tank and give the fish enough room to swim.

- Keep an eye out for any symptoms of stress or disease in your pet fish.

2. What prevalent ailments may platypus fish contract?

- Fungal illnesses, bacterial infections, parasite infestations (such as ich or flukes), and swim bladder issues are common ailments seen in platy fish.

- Stress, poor water quality, and environmental variables all have a role in the development of these disorders coming up.

3. How can I keep my platy fish healthy?

- Preserve excellent water quality by doing routine water changes and keeping an eye on temperature, ammonia, nitrite, and nitrate levels.

- To stop the spread of illness, quarantine new fish before adding them to the main fish tank.

- Refrain from overfeeding fish since uneaten food might affect the water's quality and also stress the fish.

- Maintain a stress-free environment by offering adequate tank mates, proper hiding spots, and a well cleaned surroundings.

4. What should I do in case my platy fish becomes ill?

- To stop the sickness from spreading, confine the sick fish in a different small tank.

- To choose the best course of action, do research and pinpoint the precise symptoms.

- Seek advice from a veterinarian or knowledgeable fish keeper for an accurate diagnosis and treatment strategy to take.

- Continue the recommended course of therapy until the fish has completely healed up.

- Make sure the fish have a stress-free environment while recovering and maintain proper water quality in there.

5. Can I cure platy fish illnesses with medication?

- Different drugs are available to treat different ailments in your fish.

- Pay close attention to the dose and treatment period recommendations in the medication's instructions given.

- Consult a veterinarian or knowledgeable fish keeper for advice if you're uncertain of how to proceed or step to take.

6. How can I protect my platy fish from common parasites and manage them?

- To avoid introducing any parasites, quarantine new fish before putting them in the main tank.

- Keep the water clean and stay away from crowding since stress impairs the fish's immune system.

- Keep an eye out for symptoms of parasites in your fish, such as increased scratching, changes in body color, or unusual seen behavior.

- If parasites are found, take the correct drugs or therapies that are tailored to the individual parasite and give straight away.

7. Are there any particular stress indicators in platy fish that I should look out for?

- Loss of appetite, quick or difficult breathing, increased hiding in tank, fin clamping, color changes, or strange behavior are all indications of stress in your platy fish.

- It's crucial to find and deal with the root causes of stress in them since it may make fish more prone to illness.